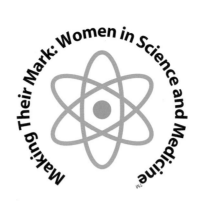

Making Their Mark: Women in Science and Medicine™

Mae Jemison
The First African American Woman Astronaut

Liza N. Burby

The Rosen Publishing Group's
PowerKids Press™
New York

Published in 1997 by The Rosen Publishing Group, Inc.
29 East 21st Street, New York, NY 10010

First Edition

Book Design: Erin McKenna

Photo Credits: front cover and pp. 11, 15, 16, 19 © UPI/Corbis-Bettmann; p. 12 © Jeffrey Jay Foxx; pp. 4, 20 © MIDWESTOCK; p. 7 © Michael P. Manheim/MIDWESTOCK; p. 8 © Mary E. Schultz/MIDWESTOCK.

Burby, Liza N.
    Mae Jemison / by Liza N. Burby
        p.   cm. — (Making their mark, women in science and medicine)
    Includes index.
    Summary: Briefly traces the life of the first African American woman to go into space, from her childhood in Chicago through her education and work as a doctor to her historic flight.
    ISBN 0-8239-5027-1 (lib. bdg.)
    1. Jemison, Mae, 1956– —Juvenile literature. 2. Afro-American women astronauts—United States—Biography—Juvenile Literature. [1. Jemison, Mae, 1956– . 2. Astronauts. 3. Afro-Americans—Biography. 4. Women—Biography.] I. Title. II. Series: Burby, Liza N. Making their mark.
TL789.J46B87 1996
629.45'0092—dc21
[B]   96-37466
                                                                                  CIP
                                                                                   AC

Contents

Dreams of Going to Space

Mae Jemison was born on October 17, 1956, in Decatur, Alabama. From the time she was young, Mae dreamed of flying to outer space. Somehow she knew she would do it, even though no woman and no African American had ever been an **astronaut** (AS-tro-not). Mae was thirteen when the *Apollo 11* spacecraft landed on the moon. It was the first time astronauts had walked on the moon. From then on, Mae read everything she could about space and **astronomy** (as-TRON-oh-me).

◀ Mae was a teenager when an astronuat first walked on the moon.

Learning from Her Father

When Mae was a little girl, her family moved from Alabama to Chicago, Illinois. She spent a lot of time with her father. They fished and hunted together. Mae also went with him to his job, where he worked as a **carpenter** (KAR-pen-ter). She learned the **skills** (SKILZ) needed to build her school science projects. From the time she spent with her father, Mae learned that she could do anything she wanted to do.

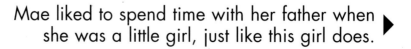
Mae liked to spend time with her father when she was a little girl, just like this girl does. ▶

Mae Studies Science

Mae liked other things besides outer space. For a while she thought she might be a dancer. But science interested her more. Even though she planned to one day work for **NASA** (NA-suh), she knew it was important to have other interests, too. She studied **chemical engineering** (KEM-ih-kul EN-jin-EER-ing) at a college in California. She also studied African and African American history.

◀ Mae knew she would one day work for NASA.

Mae Becomes a Doctor

After she graduated from college, Mae decided that she wanted to use science to help people. She went to medical school to become a doctor. While she was in school, she traveled and studied in Cuba, Africa, and Thailand. She became a doctor in 1981. She went to work in a medical center in Los Angeles, California.

Mae worked as a doctor. ▶
She liked to help people.

On the Move Again

Soon Mae was on the move again. She wanted to use what she knew about medicine and about African history to help people in Africa. When Mae was 26 years old, she joined the Peace Corps as a medical officer. She worked in poor countries with others who wanted to give people good medical care. For two and a half years, she took care of people in West African countries.

◀ Mae used what she knew about medicine to help people in African countries.

13

NASA Chooses Mae

Mae returned to the United States in 1985 to work as a doctor in California. But she had not forgotten her dream of going to space. In 1986, she was one of 2,000 people who asked NASA if they could be astronauts. One year later, she got a call from NASA. She had been chosen to become the first African American woman ever to join the astronaut training program. Mae's dream of being an astronaut was coming true.

Mae was excited that her dream was coming true. ▶

The Training Begins

Mae moved to Houston, Texas. There she began a hard year of training to be an astronaut. She learned many things, such as how to land a **space shuttle** (SPAYS SHUT-tul) in the water and how to exercise in space. She also learned how to use the special **equipment** (ee-KWIP-ment) on the space shuttle. In August 1988 she became an astronaut. She was ready to fly in a space shuttle. But she had to work at NASA for four years before she got her chance.

◄ Mae trained very hard to learn about flying in a space shuttle.

Outer Space at Last

On September 12, 1992, after years of getting ready, Mae boarded the space shuttle *Endeavour* for her first flight. Her dream had come true. She and six other astronauts took off from the Kennedy Space Center in Florida. While they were in space, they did 43 **experiments** (ex-PEER-uh-ments). One thing they wanted to learn about was space sickness. This is a kind of motion sickness that astronauts get during their first few days in space.

Mae did important work while on the space shuttle. ▶

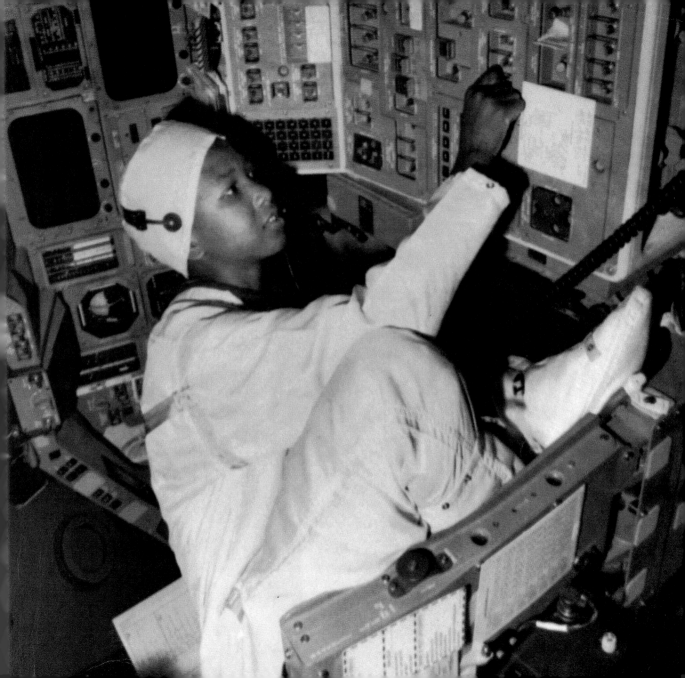

Mae Returns to Earth

On September 20, 1992, after seven days and 127 trips, or **orbits** (OR-bits) around the Earth, the *Endeavour* returned to Kennedy Space Center. Mae told reporters that the most exciting part of the trip had been looking out the window of the space shuttle and seeing planet Earth. She hoped she would be the first of many African American women to fly in space.

◀ Mae's favorite part of her trip to outer space was seeing planet Earth from the space shuttle.

Helping Others

Mae left NASA in 1993 so she could show people better ways to use science. She started the Jemison Group in Houston, Texas. This is a company that teaches people in poor countries about medicine and **technology** (tek-NOL-uh-jee). Mae believes that everyone should have the chance to make his or her dreams come true. Through her work, Mae Jemison shows people they can be anybody they want to be.

Glossary

astronaut (AS-tro-not) A person who travels to space.

astronomy (as-TRON-oh-me) The study of what is beyond planet Earth.

carpenter (KAR-pen-ter) A person who builds things as a job.

chemical engineering (KEM-ih-kul EN-jin-EER-ing) The study of how chemicals can be used to make things.

equipment (ee-KWIP-ment) Tools or supplies a person uses to do something.

experiment (ex-PEER-uh-ment) A test done to find the answer to something.

NASA (NA-suh) The National Aeronautics and Space Administration. It is the place where people study outer space and train to be astronauts.

orbit (OR-bit) The circular path a spacecraft makes around Earth.

skill (SKIL) Something a person can do very well through practice.

space shuttle (SPAYS SHUT-tul) A spacecraft used for people and equipment to move between Earth and space.

technology (tek-NOL-uh-jee)   When science is used to solve problems.

Index